Mindfulness Made Simple: A Beginner's Guide to Mental Clarity and Peace

Mindscapes: Navigating the Psyche, Volume 3

Shalna Omaye

Published by Shalna Omaye, 2024.

MINDFULNESS MADE SIMPLE: A BEGINNER'S GUIDE TO MENTAL CLARITY AND PEACE

First edition. September 3, 2024.

Copyright © 2024 Shalna Omaye.

ISBN: 979-8227016386

Written by Shalna Omaye.

To all those seeking peace in the chaos of everyday life. May this journey into mindfulness bring you clarity, compassion, and a deeper connection with yourself and the world around you.

Mindfulness
Made Simple

IN A WORLD WHERE OUR attention is constantly being pulled in multiple directions, finding peace and mental clarity can feel like an impossible task. We're often overwhelmed by the demands of work, family, and the relentless pace of modern life. Yet, amidst all this chaos, there exists a simple practice that can help us regain control, reduce stress, and live more fully in the present moment: mindfulness.

Mindfulness is the practice of bringing our full attention to the present moment, without judgment or distraction. It allows us to experience life more deeply, to connect with ourselves and others, and to navigate challenges with greater calm and clarity. While the concept of mindfulness may seem abstract, its benefits are concrete and well-documented by science—from reducing anxiety and improving mental health to enhancing focus and fostering greater overall well-being.

This book, "Mindfulness Made Simple: A Beginner's Guide to Mental Clarity and Peace," is designed to demystify mindfulness and make it accessible to everyone, regardless of your background or experience. Whether you're new to mindfulness or looking to deepen your practice, this guide will provide you with practical tools and insights to help you integrate mindfulness into your daily life.

Throughout these pages, you'll learn the basics of mindfulness, explore a variety of mindfulness techniques, and discover how to apply mindfulness in different areas of your life—from eating and working to nurturing your relationships. You'll also find tips for overcoming common challenges and staying consistent with your practice.

Mindfulness is not just a practice; it's a way of being. By embracing mindfulness, you can cultivate a sense of inner peace, clarity, and resilience that will serve you well in every aspect of your life. I invite you to approach this journey with an open mind and a willingness to explore. As you delve into the practice of mindfulness, may you find the clarity and peace you seek.

A Beginner's Guide to Mental Clarity and Peace

A BEGINNER'S GUIDE to Mental Clarity and Peace" highlights the book's focus on introducing mindfulness in a way that's accessible and easy to understand, even for those who are new to the practice. The subtitle emphasizes that through mindfulness, readers can achieve greater mental clarity—by quieting the mind and focusing on the present—and experience a deeper sense of peace in their daily lives.

Table of Contents

Chapter 9: Further Resources on Mindfulness

Chapter 1: Introduction to Mindfulness

MINDFULNESS IS A PRACTICE that has been gaining popularity in recent years, but its roots go back thousands of years. In this chapter, we'll explore what mindfulness truly is, why it has become so important in modern life, and clear up some common misconceptions that might prevent people from fully embracing its benefits. Whether you're completely new to mindfulness or just looking to deepen your understanding, this chapter will lay the foundation for the journey ahead.

1.1 What is Mindfulness?

Mindfulness is the practice of intentionally bringing your attention to the present moment with an attitude of openness and non-judgment. It's about fully engaging with whatever you're doing, whether it's something as simple as drinking a cup of tea or as complex as navigating a difficult conversation. When you practice mindfulness, you're not trying to change your thoughts or emotions, but rather to observe them as they are, without getting caught up in them.

The concept of mindfulness has its origins in ancient contemplative traditions, particularly within Buddhism, where it is a key element of meditation practice. However, mindfulness as we know it today has been adapted and popularized in the West, largely through the work of figures like Jon Kabat-Zinn, who developed the Mindfulness-Based Stress Reduction (MBSR) program in the late 1970s. This secular approach to mindfulness has made it accessible to a wide range of people, regardless of their religious or spiritual beliefs.

Mindfulness involves two key components: attention and attitude. Attention refers to the ability to focus on the present moment, while attitude refers to the way in which you approach that focus—with curiosity, openness, and acceptance. Together, these components help you develop a deeper awareness of your thoughts, emotions, and physical sensations, allowing you to respond to life's challenges with greater clarity and calm.

One of the most important aspects of mindfulness is that it is a practice. It's not something you can master overnight, but rather a skill that you develop over time with regular practice. The more you practice mindfulness, the more natural it becomes, and the greater the benefits you'll experience.

1.2 The Importance of Mindfulness in Modern Life

In today's fast-paced world, many of us live in a state of constant distraction. Our attention is pulled in multiple directions by work, family, technology, and the endless stream of information that bombards us daily. This constant state of busyness can lead to stress, anxiety, and a feeling of being overwhelmed. It can also prevent us from fully experiencing and enjoying our lives, as we're often so focused on what's next that we miss what's happening right now.

This is where mindfulness comes in. By training your mind to focus on the present moment, mindfulness helps you break free from the cycle of distraction and regain control over your attention. It allows you to slow down, observe your thoughts and feelings without judgment, and respond to situations with greater clarity and intention.

The benefits of mindfulness are well-documented. Research has shown that regular mindfulness practice can reduce stress, improve mental health, enhance focus and concentration, and increase overall well-being. It can also help you develop a greater sense of self-awareness, which is key to understanding your patterns of thought and behavior and making positive changes in your life.

Mindfulness is particularly important in modern life because it offers a way to navigate the complexities and challenges of the world with greater ease and resilience. It helps you stay grounded in the present, even when life gets hectic, and provides you with the tools to manage your emotions and reactions more effectively. In short, mindfulness can help you live a more balanced, peaceful, and fulfilling life.

1.3 Debunking Myths About Mindfulness

Despite its growing popularity, there are still many misconceptions about mindfulness that can prevent people from fully embracing the practice. Let's take a moment to address some of the most common myths:

Myth 1: Mindfulness Is About Emptying Your Mind of Thoughts

One of the biggest misconceptions about mindfulness is that it requires you to clear your mind of all thoughts. In reality, mindfulness is not about stopping your thoughts, but about observing them without getting caught up in them. It's natural for the mind to produce thoughts—this is what minds do. The goal of mindfulness is to notice these thoughts as they arise and let them pass without judgment or attachment.

Myth 2: Mindfulness Is Only for Meditation

While mindfulness is often associated with meditation, it's not limited to formal meditation practice. Mindfulness can be practiced in any moment of your day, whether you're eating, walking, working, or even brushing your teeth. The key is to bring your full attention to whatever you're doing and to approach it with a sense of curiosity and openness.

Myth 3: Mindfulness Is a Religious Practice

Although mindfulness has roots in Buddhist meditation, the practice itself is secular and can be embraced by people of any or no religious background. Mindfulness is simply a way of training the mind to focus on the present moment and to respond to life with greater awareness and compassion. It's a practice that can complement any belief system or lifestyle.

Myth 4: Mindfulness Takes Too Much Time

Many people believe that they don't have time to practice mindfulness, but the reality is that mindfulness can be integrated into your daily routine without taking up extra time. You don't need to set aside hours each day to meditate—just a few minutes of mindful breathing or a short mindful pause during your day can make a significant difference. Additionally, you can practice mindfulness while doing other activities, such as eating or walking, making it a flexible and accessible practice.

Myth 5: Mindfulness Is About Being Passive

Another common misconception is that mindfulness is about being passive or accepting everything without taking action. In truth, mindfulness is about developing a clear and balanced awareness that allows you to respond to situations with greater wisdom and effectiveness. It's not about avoiding problems or letting things slide, but about approaching life's challenges with a calm and focused mind.

By debunking these myths, we hope to clarify what mindfulness really is and make it more approachable for everyone. As you continue through this book, you'll learn how to integrate mindfulness into your life in a way that feels natural and beneficial, without the pressure of unrealistic expectations.

Chapter 2: The Basics of Mindfulness Practice

NOW THAT YOU UNDERSTAND what mindfulness is and why it's important, it's time to dive into the basics of how to practice it. In this chapter, we'll explore the fundamental principles that form the foundation of mindfulness. You'll learn about the mind-body connection, the art of paying attention, and simple breathing techniques that can help you start your mindfulness journey. These basics will set the stage for the more detailed practices and techniques discussed in later chapters.

2.1 Understanding the Mind-Body Connection

The mind-body connection is a central concept in mindfulness practice. It refers to the idea that our mental and emotional states are closely linked to our physical sensations and behaviors, and vice versa. When you're stressed or anxious, for example, you might notice physical symptoms such as a racing heart, tense muscles, or shallow breathing. Similarly, when you're physically relaxed, your mind tends to be calmer and more focused.

Mindfulness leverages this connection by encouraging you to become more aware of your physical sensations as a way to anchor your attention in the present moment. By paying close attention to your body—whether it's the feeling of your breath as it moves in and out, the sensation of your feet on the ground as you walk, or the tension in your shoulders during a stressful moment—you can better understand how your mental state is influencing your physical experience.

One of the key benefits of focusing on the body in mindfulness practice is that it helps to ground you in the here and now. Our minds are often scattered, jumping from one thought to the next, dwelling on the past, or worrying about the future. But the body is always present, providing a constant and reliable anchor for your attention.

As you begin your mindfulness practice, try to develop a habit of regularly checking in with your body. Notice how you're feeling physically throughout the day, especially during moments of stress or distraction. This simple act of awareness can help you stay grounded and connected to the present moment, which is the essence of mindfulness.

2.2 The Art of Paying Attention

At the heart of mindfulness is the practice of paying attention—deliberately, fully, and without judgment. This may sound simple, but in reality, it can be quite challenging. Our minds are naturally prone to wander, and in today's fast-paced world, it's easy to get caught up in distractions, multitasking, and the constant influx of information.

The art of paying attention in mindfulness involves several key elements:

Intention: Mindful attention is purposeful. You choose to focus on the present moment, whether it's your breath, your body, or your surroundings. This intention is what sets mindfulness apart from the mind's usual habit of drifting aimlessly from thought to thought.

Awareness: Mindfulness is about being fully aware of whatever you're focusing on. If you're paying attention to your breath, for example, you notice the subtle sensations of the air moving in and out of your nostrils, the rise and fall of your chest, and the feeling of the breath filling your lungs. This heightened awareness helps you connect more deeply with your experience.

Non-judgment: When practicing mindfulness, it's important to observe your experience without judgment. This means letting go of any labels or evaluations you might place on your thoughts, emotions, or sensations.

Instead of thinking, "I'm so tense, this is bad," you simply notice the tension in your body without attaching a value judgment to it. This non-judgmental attitude creates a sense of openness and acceptance, allowing you to experience the present moment more fully.

Curiosity: Approach your mindfulness practice with a sense of curiosity and exploration. Each moment is unique, and by cultivating a beginner's mind—an attitude of openness and eagerness to see things as if for the first time—you can discover new aspects of your experience that you might otherwise overlook.

To practice the art of paying attention, start with small, everyday activities. Choose a simple task, like washing the dishes, drinking a cup of tea, or taking a walk, and try to give it your full attention. Notice the sights, sounds, smells, and physical sensations associated with the activity. If your mind starts to wander, gently bring it back to the present moment. The more you practice, the more skilled you'll become at maintaining your attention, even in the midst of distractions.

2.3 Breathing Techniques for Beginners

Breathing is one of the most accessible and effective anchors for mindfulness practice. Because your breath is always with you, it's a convenient and powerful tool for bringing your attention back to the present moment whenever your mind starts to wander.

Here are a few simple breathing techniques that can help you begin your mindfulness practice:

Mindful Breathing:

- Find a comfortable position, either sitting or lying down.
- Close your eyes if that feels comfortable for you.
- Bring your attention to your breath. Notice the sensation of the

air as it enters and leaves your nostrils, the rise and fall of your chest, or the movement of your abdomen.

- Simply observe your breath without trying to change it. Allow your breathing to flow naturally.
- If your mind starts to wander, gently bring your attention back to your breath.
- Practice this for a few minutes, gradually increasing the time as you become more comfortable.

Counting Breaths:

- Sit comfortably with your back straight and your eyes closed.
- Begin by taking a few deep breaths to settle in.
- On your next exhale, silently count "one." On the next exhale, count "two," and so on, up to ten.
- If you lose count or your mind wanders, start again from one.
- This simple technique helps to keep your focus on your breath and provides a gentle structure for your practice.

Box Breathing (Four-Square Breathing):

- Find a comfortable position and close your eyes.
- Inhale slowly through your nose for a count of four.
- Hold your breath for a count of four.
- Exhale slowly through your mouth for a count of four.
- Hold your breath again for a count of four.
- Repeat this cycle for several minutes.
- Box breathing is particularly useful for calming the mind and body, making it a great technique for reducing stress and anxiety.

Breath Awareness with Body Scan:

- Sit or lie down comfortably and close your eyes.
- Begin by taking a few deep breaths to center yourself.
- As you continue to breathe naturally, bring your attention to different parts of your body, starting with your toes and working your way up to your head.
- Notice any sensations in each area—tension, warmth, coolness, or tingling—while continuing to focus on your breath.
- This technique combines breath awareness with a body scan, helping you to connect with both your breath and your physical sensations.

These breathing techniques are simple yet powerful tools for cultivating mindfulness. They can be practiced anywhere and at any time, making them an ideal starting point for beginners. As you become more comfortable with these techniques, you can integrate them into your daily routine and use them as a foundation for more advanced mindfulness practices.

Chapter 3: Mindfulness Techniques and Exercises

Now that you've learned the basics of mindfulness practice, it's time to explore specific techniques and exercises that can help you cultivate mindfulness in your daily life. In this chapter, you'll find step-by-step guides to some of the most effective mindfulness practices, from mindful breathing and body scan meditation to mindful walking and loving-kindness meditation. These exercises are designed to help you deepen your practice, reduce stress, and develop greater self-awareness and compassion.

3.1 Mindful Breathing: A Step-by-Step Guide

Mindful breathing is one of the most fundamental and accessible mindfulness practices. It involves paying close attention to your breath as it moves in and out of your body, helping you stay grounded in the present moment. This practice is simple yet powerful, offering a way to calm your mind, reduce stress, and cultivate a sense of inner peace.

Step-by-Step Guide to Mindful Breathing:

Find a Comfortable Position:

- Sit in a chair with your feet flat on the floor, or sit cross-legged on a cushion. You can also lie down if that's more comfortable.
- Keep your back straight but relaxed, allowing your body to be alert yet at ease.
- Rest your hands on your lap or by your sides.

Close Your Eyes:

- If you feel comfortable doing so, gently close your eyes. This helps minimize distractions and allows you to focus more fully on your breath.

Bring Your Attention to Your Breath:

- Begin by taking a few deep breaths, inhaling through your nose and exhaling through your mouth.
- Allow your breath to settle into its natural rhythm, without trying to control it.
- Focus your attention on the sensation of your breath as it enters and leaves your body. Notice the coolness of the air as you inhale and the warmth as you exhale.

Observe Without Judgment:

- As you continue to breathe, simply observe your breath without trying to change it. If your mind starts to wander, gently bring your attention back to your breath.
- Notice how your body moves with each breath—the rise and fall of your chest, the expansion and contraction of your abdomen.
- Allow yourself to be fully present with each breath, letting go of any thoughts, worries, or distractions.

Practice for a Few Minutes:

- Continue this practice for several minutes, gradually increasing the duration as you become more comfortable.
- If your mind wanders, gently guide it back to your breath without judgment. Remember, the goal is not to stop your thoughts but to observe them and return to the present moment.

Gently End the Practice:

- When you're ready to end your practice, take a few deep breaths and slowly open your eyes.
- Take a moment to notice how you feel—physically, mentally, and emotionally.
- Carry this sense of mindfulness with you as you continue with your day.

Mindful breathing can be practiced anywhere and at any time, making it a versatile tool for managing stress and staying present. Whether you have just a few minutes or a longer period to dedicate to this practice, mindful breathing is a simple yet profound way to cultivate mindfulness.

3.2 Body Scan Meditation: Reconnecting with Your Body

The body scan meditation is a powerful mindfulness technique that helps you reconnect with your body and develop greater awareness of physical sensations. This practice involves systematically focusing your attention on different parts of your body, noticing any sensations, tension, or discomfort without judgment. The body scan is particularly effective for releasing physical tension and promoting relaxation.

Step-by-Step Guide to Body Scan Meditation:

Find a Comfortable Position:

- Lie down on your back with your arms resting by your sides and your legs extended. You can also sit in a chair if lying down isn't comfortable for you.
- Close your eyes and allow your body to relax.

Take a Few Deep Breaths:

- Begin by taking a few deep breaths, inhaling through your nose and exhaling through your mouth.
- With each exhale, allow your body to sink deeper into relaxation.

Focus on Your Toes:

- Bring your attention to your toes. Notice any sensations you feel in this area, such as warmth, coolness, tingling, or tension.
- Spend a few moments simply observing these sensations without trying to change them.

Move Up Through Your Body:

- Gradually move your attention up through your body, focusing on each part in turn. After your toes, move to your feet, ankles, calves, knees, thighs, and so on.
- As you focus on each area, notice any sensations—tightness, relaxation, pain, or comfort.
- If you encounter areas of tension, imagine sending your breath to those areas, allowing them to soften and relax with each exhale.

Continue Up to Your Head:

- Continue moving your attention through your torso, chest, back, shoulders, arms, hands, neck, and finally your head.
- Pay attention to your face, jaw, and scalp, noticing any areas of tension or relaxation.

Observe Without Judgment:

- Throughout the body scan, maintain a non-judgmental

attitude. There's no need to analyze or fix anything—just observe whatever sensations arise with curiosity and acceptance.

Complete the Body Scan:

- Once you've scanned your entire body, take a few deep breaths and notice how your body feels as a whole.
- Slowly open your eyes and take a moment to reorient yourself before getting up.

The body scan meditation is a wonderful practice for developing a deeper connection with your body and releasing physical tension. It can be especially helpful before bed to promote relaxation and improve sleep.

3.3 Mindful Walking: Bringing Awareness to Movement

Mindful walking is a practice that combines movement with mindfulness, allowing you to bring awareness to the simple act of walking. This technique is particularly useful for those who find it challenging to sit still for meditation. By focusing on the sensations of walking, you can cultivate mindfulness while staying physically active.

Step-by-Step Guide to Mindful Walking:

Choose a Location:

- Find a quiet, safe place where you can walk without distractions. This could be a park, a quiet street, or even a hallway in your home.

Stand Still and Breathe:

- Before you start walking, stand still for a moment and take a few deep breaths. Allow yourself to fully arrive in the present moment.

Begin Walking Slowly:

- Start walking at a slow, deliberate pace. Pay attention to each step, noticing how your foot lifts off the ground, moves forward, and then makes contact with the ground again.
- Focus on the sensations in your feet—how they feel as they touch the ground, the shifting of weight from one foot to the other, and the movement of your legs.

Engage All Your Senses:

- As you walk, bring your attention to your surroundings. Notice the sights, sounds, and smells around you. Feel the breeze on your skin, the warmth of the sun, or the coolness of the air.
- If your mind starts to wander, gently bring it back to the physical sensations of walking.

Coordinate Breathing with Steps:

- You can enhance your mindful walking practice by coordinating your breathing with your steps. For example, inhale for four steps and exhale for four steps, or find a rhythm that feels natural to you.

Practice for Several Minutes:

- Continue walking mindfully for several minutes or longer, depending on the time you have available. You can walk in a straight line, in circles, or along a path—whatever suits your environment.

Conclude Your Practice:

- When you're ready to finish, gradually slow your pace and come to a stop. Take a moment to stand still, breathe deeply, and reflect on how you feel.
- Carry this sense of mindfulness with you as you transition back into your regular activities.

Mindful walking is a versatile practice that can be done almost anywhere. It's a great way to incorporate mindfulness into your day, especially if you're someone who enjoys being active.

3.4 Loving-Kindness Meditation: Cultivating Compassion

Loving-kindness meditation, also known as metta meditation, is a practice that focuses on cultivating feelings of compassion and goodwill toward yourself and others. This meditation involves silently repeating phrases of well-wishing, first directed toward yourself and then extended to others, including loved ones, acquaintances, and even those with whom you have difficulties.

Step-by-Step Guide to Loving-Kindness Meditation:

Find a Comfortable Position:

- Sit in a comfortable position with your back straight and your eyes closed.
- Rest your hands in your lap or on your knees.

Begin with Yourself:

- Start by directing loving-kindness toward yourself. Silently repeat phrases such as:
- "May I be happy."

- "May I be healthy."
- "May I be safe."
- "May I live with ease."
- As you repeat these phrases, try to connect with the feelings of warmth and compassion that they invoke.

Extend to a Loved One:

- Next, bring to mind someone you care about deeply. Visualize this person in your mind and silently repeat the same phrases, directing them toward your loved one:
- "May you be happy."
- "May you be healthy."
- "May you be safe."
- "May you live with ease."
- Feel the sense of loving-kindness expanding outward as you send these wishes to your loved one.

Extend to a Neutral Person:

- Now, think of someone you know but don't have strong feelings toward—perhaps a colleague or an acquaintance. Visualize this person and repeat the phrases:
- "May you be happy."
- "May you be healthy."
- "May you be safe."
- "May you live with ease."
- Notice how it feels to extend loving-kindness to someone you feel neutral about.

Extend to Someone with Whom You Have Difficulties:

- This step can be challenging, but it's a powerful part of the practice. Bring to mind someone with whom you have difficulties or conflict. Visualize this person and silently repeat the phrases:

- "May you be happy."
- "May you be healthy."
- "May you be safe."
- "May you live with ease."
- Try to let go of any negative feelings and focus on the intention of wishing this person well.

Extend to All Beings:

- Finally, broaden your focus to include all living beings everywhere. Silently repeat the phrases:
- "May all beings be happy."
- "May all beings be healthy."
- "May all beings be safe."
- "May all beings live with ease."
- Feel the sense of loving-kindness radiating out to encompass the entire world.

Conclude Your Practice:

- When you're ready, take a few deep breaths and slowly open your eyes.
- Take a moment to reflect on how you feel, noticing any sense of warmth, compassion, or openness in your heart.

Loving-kindness meditation is a beautiful practice for cultivating compassion and empathy, both for yourself and others. It can help soften feelings of anger, resentment, or isolation and create a deeper sense of connection with the world around you.

Chapter 4: The Benefits of Mindfulness

Mindfulness is not just a practice; it's a gateway to a multitude of benefits that can transform your mental, emotional, and physical well-being. In this chapter, we'll explore the many advantages of mindfulness, from reducing stress and anxiety to enhancing focus and mental clarity. You'll discover how mindfulness can improve emotional regulation, boost overall well-being, and even positively impact your relationships and professional life.

4.1 Reducing Stress and Anxiety

One of the most well-documented benefits of mindfulness is its ability to reduce stress and anxiety. In today's fast-paced world, stress has become a common experience, and chronic stress can lead to a range of physical and mental health issues. Mindfulness offers a powerful tool for managing stress by helping you break the cycle of anxious thoughts and return to the present moment.

When you practice mindfulness, you train your mind to focus on what is happening right now, rather than getting caught up in worries about the future or regrets about the past. This shift in focus can significantly reduce the mental chatter that often fuels anxiety. By observing your thoughts without judgment and letting them pass without reacting, you create a sense of calm and perspective.

Research has shown that regular mindfulness practice can lower levels of the stress hormone cortisol, reduce symptoms of anxiety disorders, and increase resilience to stress. Techniques such as mindful breathing, body scan meditation, and mindful walking can be particularly effective in calming the nervous system and promoting relaxation.

In addition to these immediate effects, mindfulness also helps you develop long-term strategies for managing stress. By becoming more aware of your stress triggers and habitual reactions, you can begin to respond to challenges with greater clarity and composure. Over time, mindfulness can help you cultivate a more balanced and peaceful approach to life, reducing the impact of stress and anxiety on your overall well-being.

4.2 Enhancing Focus and Mental Clarity

In a world filled with distractions, maintaining focus and mental clarity can be challenging. Whether it's the constant influx of emails, social media notifications, or the demands of multitasking, it's easy to feel scattered and overwhelmed. Mindfulness offers a way to sharpen your focus and enhance mental clarity by training your mind to stay present and engaged.

When you practice mindfulness, you develop the ability to direct your attention where it's needed and to sustain that focus over time. This skill is particularly valuable in both personal and professional settings, where the ability to concentrate can significantly impact your productivity and decision-making.

Mindfulness improves focus by encouraging you to bring your attention back to the present moment whenever your mind starts to wander. For example, in mindful breathing, each time you notice your thoughts drifting, you gently guide them back to your breath. This repeated practice strengthens your mental muscles, making it easier to concentrate on tasks and resist distractions.

Mental clarity is another key benefit of mindfulness. When your mind is clear, you're better able to think critically, solve problems, and make decisions. Mindfulness helps clear the mental fog that often accompanies stress, anxiety, or overthinking. By focusing on the present moment, you reduce the mental clutter that can cloud your judgment, allowing you to approach situations with greater insight and perspective.

Studies have shown that mindfulness can enhance cognitive functions such as attention, memory, and problem-solving skills. Whether you're preparing for an important presentation, working on a creative project, or simply trying to manage your daily tasks more effectively, mindfulness can help you stay focused, think more clearly, and achieve your goals with greater ease.

4.3 Improving Emotional Regulation

Emotional regulation is the ability to manage and respond to your emotions in a healthy and constructive way. It's a crucial skill for maintaining mental and emotional well-being, and mindfulness can play a significant role in enhancing this ability.

Mindfulness helps improve emotional regulation by increasing your awareness of your emotions as they arise. Instead of being swept away by intense feelings or reacting impulsively, mindfulness allows you to observe your emotions with curiosity and non-judgment. This awareness creates a space between the emotion and your reaction, giving you the opportunity to choose how to respond.

For example, if you're feeling angry or frustrated, mindfulness can help you recognize these emotions before they escalate. By taking a mindful pause—perhaps through deep breathing or a quick body scan—you can calm your nervous system and approach the situation with a clearer mind. This mindful response can prevent you from saying or doing something in the heat of the moment that you might later regret.

Mindfulness also fosters greater emotional resilience. By regularly practicing mindfulness, you develop the capacity to handle difficult emotions with more ease and stability. You become more adept at letting go of negative emotions and moving on from challenging experiences without getting stuck in rumination or resentment.

Additionally, mindfulness can help you cultivate positive emotions such as gratitude, compassion, and joy. Practices like loving-kindness meditation are specifically designed to enhance feelings of warmth and goodwill toward yourself and others. By nurturing these positive emotions, you can create a more balanced and fulfilling emotional life.

Overall, mindfulness empowers you to navigate your emotional landscape with greater skill and grace. Whether you're dealing with stress, anxiety, anger, or sadness, mindfulness provides the tools to manage your emotions effectively and maintain a sense of inner peace.

4.4 Boosting Overall Well-Being

The benefits of mindfulness extend beyond mental and emotional health to encompass overall well-being. Regular mindfulness practice has been shown to have positive effects on physical health, relationships, and overall life satisfaction.

Physical Health:

Mindfulness can contribute to better physical health by reducing stress-related symptoms such as high blood pressure, chronic pain, and insomnia. The practice of mindfulness has also been linked to a stronger immune system, improved digestion, and reduced inflammation. By promoting relaxation and reducing the physiological effects of stress, mindfulness can help you maintain a healthier body and prevent illness.

Relationships:

Mindfulness can enhance your relationships by improving your ability to communicate, empathize, and connect with others. When you practice mindfulness, you become more present and attentive in your interactions, which can lead to deeper and more meaningful connections. Mindfulness also helps you navigate conflicts with greater understanding and compassion, fostering healthier and more harmonious relationships.

Life Satisfaction:

Mindfulness can increase your overall sense of well-being by helping you appreciate the present moment and find joy in everyday experiences. By cultivating an attitude of gratitude and acceptance, mindfulness allows you to let go of the constant striving for more and to find contentment in the here and now. This shift in perspective can lead to greater life satisfaction and a deeper sense of fulfillment.

Research has shown that people who practice mindfulness regularly report higher levels of happiness, lower levels of depression, and a greater sense of purpose in life. Whether you're looking to improve your physical health, enhance your relationships, or simply feel more content and at peace, mindfulness offers a path to greater overall well-being.

Chapter 5: Integrating Mindfulness into Daily Life

Mindfulness is not just something you practice for a few minutes each day—it's a way of being that can permeate every aspect of your life. In this chapter, we'll explore how to integrate mindfulness into your daily routines, from eating and working to nurturing relationships. You'll learn practical tips for bringing mindfulness into everyday activities, helping you stay present, reduce stress, and enhance your overall well-being.

5.1 Mindful Eating: Savoring Every Bite

Eating is something we do every day, yet it's often done mindlessly—while watching TV, scrolling through our phones, or rushing through a meal to get to the next task. Mindful eating offers a way to transform this routine activity into a deeply nourishing experience for both body and mind.

What is Mindful Eating? Mindful eating is the practice of bringing full attention to the process of eating. It involves being fully present with your food, from the moment you prepare it to the moment you take the last bite. By eating mindfully, you engage all your senses—sight, smell, taste, and even sound—allowing you to fully savor each bite and appreciate the nourishment your food provides.

How to Practice Mindful Eating:

Set the Stage:

- Begin by creating a calm and pleasant environment for your meal. Turn off distractions like TV or smartphones, and take a moment to appreciate the food in front of you.

- Consider expressing gratitude for the food you're about to eat, acknowledging the effort that went into its preparation and the nourishment it will provide.

Engage Your Senses:

- Before taking your first bite, take a moment to look at your food. Notice the colors, shapes, and textures.

- Bring the food close to your nose and inhale its aroma. What scents do you notice?
- As you take your first bite, pay attention to the flavors, textures, and temperatures in your mouth. Chew slowly, savoring each bite.
- Notice how your body feels as you eat—how the food feels as it travels down your throat, the sensation of fullness in your stomach.

Eat Slowly and Mindfully:

- Take small bites and chew your food thoroughly. This not only aids digestion but also allows you to fully experience the taste and texture of your food.
- Put down your utensils between bites and take a moment to breathe. This helps prevent overeating and allows you to listen to your body's hunger and fullness cues.

Notice Your Body's Signals:

- Throughout the meal, pay attention to how your body feels. Are you still hungry, or are you starting to feel full? Mindful eating helps you tune into your body's natural signals, which can prevent overeating and promote healthier eating habits.

- Stop eating when you feel satisfied, even if there's still food on your plate. Mindful eating is about honoring your body's needs, not adhering to external cues like finishing everything on your plate.

Reflect on the Experience:

- After the meal, take a moment to reflect on how you feel. Are you satisfied and energized? Did you enjoy the experience of eating mindfully?
- Consider how mindful eating differs from your usual eating habits and how it might impact your relationship with food.

Mindful eating not only enhances your enjoyment of food but also helps you develop a healthier relationship with eating. By paying attention to what and how you eat, you can make more conscious choices that support your well-being.

5.2 Mindfulness at Work: Staying Present Amidst Busyness

Work can be a major source of stress, especially when deadlines loom, and the demands keep piling up. However, bringing mindfulness into your workday can help you stay calm, focused, and productive, even in the midst of busyness.

What is Mindfulness at Work? Mindfulness at work involves bringing the same principles of mindfulness—presence, attention, and non-judgment—to your tasks and interactions throughout the day. Whether you're working on a project, attending a meeting, or interacting with colleagues, practicing mindfulness can help you stay centered and engaged.

How to Practice Mindfulness at Work:

Start Your Day Mindfully:

- Before diving into your to-do list, take a few moments to set an intention for the day. This could be something like "Today, I will approach my work with focus and calm" or "I will practice patience and kindness in my interactions."
- Take a few deep breaths and visualize how you want your day to unfold.

Focus on One Task at a Time:

- Multitasking can lead to mistakes and increase stress. Instead, try to focus on one task at a time, giving it your full attention.
- If your mind starts to wander, gently bring it back to the task at hand. Use your breath as an anchor to stay present.

Take Mindful Breaks:

- Throughout the day, take short breaks to reset and recharge. This could be as simple as standing up to stretch, taking a few deep breaths, or going for a short walk.
- During these breaks, allow yourself to fully disconnect from work. This helps prevent burnout and keeps your mind sharp.

Practice Mindful Listening:

- In meetings or conversations, practice mindful listening by giving the speaker your full attention. Resist the urge to interrupt or start thinking about your response before the person has finished speaking.
- Focus on understanding the speaker's message, and reflect back

what you've heard to ensure clarity.

Respond Rather Than React:

- Work can sometimes involve stressful situations or challenging interactions. When faced with stress, pause and take a deep breath before responding. This helps you respond with intention rather than reacting impulsively.
- Consider your words and actions carefully, and approach challenges with a calm and open mind.

End Your Day with Reflection:

- At the end of the workday, take a few minutes to reflect on how the day went. What went well? What challenges did you face? How did you handle them?
- Use this reflection to identify areas where you can bring more mindfulness into your work and to acknowledge your efforts in staying present and focused.

By integrating mindfulness into your workday, you can reduce stress, improve your focus, and enhance your overall job satisfaction. Mindfulness helps you approach work with greater clarity and purpose, making your workday more fulfilling and less overwhelming.

5.3 Mindfulness in Relationships: Deepening Connections

Relationships are a vital part of our lives, but they can also be a source of stress and conflict if not nurtured with care. Mindfulness can play a transformative role in improving communication, deepening connections, and fostering a sense of understanding and empathy in your relationships.

What is Mindfulness in Relationships? Mindfulness in relationships involves bringing awareness, presence, and non-judgment to your interactions with others. It means being fully present with the people you care about, listening deeply, and responding with compassion. Practicing mindfulness in relationships can help you connect more authentically and navigate challenges with greater ease.

How to Practice Mindfulness in Relationships:

Be Present with Others:

- When spending time with loved ones, give them your full attention. Put away distractions like phones or laptops, and focus on being fully engaged in the conversation or activity.
- Practice active listening by really hearing what the other person is saying without planning your response or getting distracted by your thoughts.

Communicate with Compassion:

- Approach your conversations with an open heart and mind. Speak honestly but kindly, and be mindful of your tone and body language.
- If a conflict arises, take a moment to breathe before responding. This helps you stay calm and prevents you from reacting impulsively.

Practice Gratitude:

- Regularly express gratitude for the people in your life. Let them know what you appreciate about them and how much they mean to you.
- Gratitude can strengthen your relationships by fostering a

positive and appreciative atmosphere.

Mindful Touch:

- Physical touch can be a powerful way to connect with others. When appropriate, practice mindful touch by being fully present in the moment, whether it's a hug, a handshake, or a pat on the back.
- Notice the sensations of touch and the emotions it evokes, deepening your connection with the other person.

Mindful Conflict Resolution:

- Conflict is a natural part of any relationship, but how you handle it can make all the difference. When conflicts arise, approach them with mindfulness by staying calm, listening to the other person's perspective, and expressing your feelings clearly and respectfully.
- Aim for a resolution that honors both parties' needs and feelings, rather than trying to "win" the argument.

Reflect on Your Relationships:

- Take time to regularly reflect on your relationships. Consider what's going well and what areas might need more attention or care.
- Use this reflection to identify ways to bring more mindfulness into your interactions and to nurture your connections.

By practicing mindfulness in your relationships, you can deepen your connections, improve communication, and create a more loving and supportive environment for both yourself and those you care about.

5.4 Creating a Daily Mindfulness Routine

Consistency is key to reaping the benefits of mindfulness, and establishing a daily mindfulness routine can help you maintain and deepen your practice. Whether you have a few minutes or more time to dedicate each day, incorporating mindfulness into your routine can enhance your well-being and help you stay grounded throughout the day.

How to Create a Daily Mindfulness Routine:

Start Small:

- Begin with a manageable amount of time, such as 5-10 minutes each day. As you become more comfortable with your practice, you can gradually increase the time.
- Choose a specific time of day to practice mindfulness, whether it's in the morning to start your day, during a lunch break, or in the evening to unwind.

Incorporate a Variety of Practices:

- Your mindfulness routine can include a mix of different practices, such as mindful breathing, meditation, mindful walking, or body scan meditation.
- Experiment with different techniques to find what resonates with you and fits into your lifestyle.

Create a Dedicated Space:

- If possible, designate a specific area in your home for your mindfulness practice. This could be a quiet corner with a comfortable cushion, a chair, or even a spot in your garden.
- Having a dedicated space can help signal to your mind and body that it's time to focus on mindfulness.

Use Reminders:

- Incorporate mindfulness reminders into your daily routine. This could be as simple as setting an alarm on your phone, placing sticky notes in key areas, or using a mindfulness app that sends you reminders throughout the day.
- These reminders can help you stay consistent and bring your attention back to the present moment, even on busy days.

Integrate Mindfulness into Everyday Activities:

- Mindfulness doesn't have to be limited to formal practice. Look for opportunities to bring mindfulness into your everyday activities, such as mindful eating, mindful driving, or practicing mindfulness while doing household chores.

This approach allows you to stay connected to the present moment throughout the day, even when you're not sitting in meditation.

End Your Day with Mindfulness:

- Consider incorporating mindfulness into your evening routine to help you unwind and prepare for a restful night's sleep. This could involve a short meditation, mindful breathing, or a body scan to release any tension from the day.
- Reflect on your day with gratitude, acknowledging the moments of mindfulness you experienced and setting an intention for the next day.

Be Kind to Yourself:

- Remember that mindfulness is a practice, and it's okay if some days are more challenging than others. If you miss a day or find it difficult to focus, be kind to yourself and gently return to your practice the next day.

- Consistency is important, but so is self-compassion. Approach your mindfulness routine with patience and a willingness to learn and grow.

By creating a daily mindfulness routine, you can build a strong foundation for your practice and integrate mindfulness into all aspects of your life. This routine will support your mental, emotional, and physical well-being, helping you stay grounded, focused, and present in the midst of life's demands.

Chapter 6: Overcoming Challenges in Mindfulness Practice

Mindfulness is a valuable practice, but like any skill, it comes with its own set of challenges. Whether you're new to mindfulness or have been practicing for some time, you may encounter obstacles such as restlessness, distraction, doubt, or inconsistency. In this chapter, we'll explore common challenges in mindfulness practice and offer practical strategies for overcoming them. By addressing these challenges head-on, you can deepen your practice and experience the full benefits of mindfulness.

6.1 Dealing with Restlessness and Distraction

Restlessness and distraction are common hurdles in mindfulness practice, particularly in the beginning. The mind is naturally prone to wander, and sitting still for meditation or focusing on the present moment can feel challenging, especially if you're used to being constantly active or multitasking.

Understanding Restlessness and Distraction: Restlessness often arises from an inability to sit still or a feeling of impatience, as if you need to be doing something else. Distraction, on the other hand, is when your mind drifts away from the present moment, leading you to focus on thoughts, worries, or external stimuli.

Strategies for Overcoming Restlessness and Distraction:

Acknowledge the Distraction:

- The first step in dealing with distraction is to simply acknowledge it. When you notice that your mind has wandered, gently bring your attention back to the present moment, whether it's your breath, your body, or the task at hand.

- Avoid judging yourself for becoming distracted. It's a natural part of the process, and every time you bring your attention back, you're strengthening your mindfulness practice.

Start with Short Sessions:

- If sitting still for long periods feels overwhelming, start with shorter mindfulness sessions. Even a few minutes of mindful breathing or meditation can be effective. Gradually increase the duration as you become more comfortable with the practice.

- You can also incorporate mindfulness into activities that involve movement, such as mindful walking or yoga, which can help reduce restlessness.

Use a Physical Anchor:

- Focusing on a physical sensation, such as your breath, the feeling of your feet on the ground, or the movement of your hands, can help ground you in the present moment. This physical anchor provides a point of focus that can help reduce restlessness and keep your mind from wandering.

- If restlessness persists, try incorporating deep breathing or progressive muscle relaxation to help calm your body and mind.

Accept Restlessness as Part of the Process:

- Recognize that restlessness and distraction are normal parts of the mindfulness journey. Instead of fighting these sensations, accept them with a sense of curiosity and openness. Ask yourself what might be causing the restlessness and use it as an opportunity for self-reflection.

- Over time, you'll likely find that these sensations become less intense as you develop greater comfort with stillness and presence.

Incorporate Movement into Your Practice:

- If sitting still is particularly challenging, consider incorporating mindful movement into your practice. Activities like mindful walking, yoga, or tai chi allow you to stay active while practicing mindfulness, helping you channel restlessness into focused movement.

By acknowledging restlessness and distraction and applying these strategies, you can gradually overcome these challenges and deepen your mindfulness practice. Remember, patience and persistence are key, and each time you bring your attention back to the present moment, you're making progress.

6.2 Addressing Doubts and Misconceptions

As you continue your mindfulness journey, it's natural to encounter doubts or misconceptions about the practice. These doubts can stem from unrealistic expectations, frustration with progress, or misunderstandings about what mindfulness truly involves.

Common Doubts and Misconceptions:

"I'm Not Doing It Right":

- One of the most common doubts is the fear that you're not practicing mindfulness correctly. You might worry that you're not reaching a certain state of calm or that your mind is too distracted.
- Overcoming the Doubt: Remember that mindfulness is not

about achieving perfection or reaching a specific state of mind. It's about being present and aware, regardless of what thoughts or emotions arise. There is no "right" or "wrong" way to practice mindfulness—what matters is that you're showing up and being present with your experience.

"I Don't Have Time for This":

- Another common doubt is the belief that you're too busy to practice mindfulness, especially if you have a hectic schedule or a lot of responsibilities.
- Overcoming the Doubt: Mindfulness doesn't require hours of meditation each day. Even just a few minutes of mindful breathing, mindful eating, or taking a mindful pause during your day can have significant benefits. Consider how you might integrate mindfulness into your existing routine rather than seeing it as something extra.

"Mindfulness Isn't Working for Me":

- Some people may feel that mindfulness isn't providing the immediate results they expected, leading to frustration or doubt about the effectiveness of the practice.
- Overcoming the Doubt: Mindfulness is a gradual process, and its benefits often unfold over time. It's important to approach mindfulness with patience and an open mind. Reflect on the small changes you've noticed—perhaps in your stress levels, emotional regulation, or ability to focus—and recognize that progress is often subtle but cumulative.

"Mindfulness Is Just a Trend":

- You might encounter the misconception that mindfulness is

just a passing trend, and therefore not worth investing time in.

Overcoming the Doubt:

- Mindfulness has been practiced for thousands of years and is supported by a growing body of scientific research. Its benefits are well-documented, and many people have found it to be a valuable tool for enhancing their well-being. Consider exploring the research and reading about the experiences of others who have benefited from mindfulness to reinforce its value.

"I'm Too Distracted to Meditate":

- If you find it difficult to focus during meditation, you might doubt your ability to practice mindfulness effectively.
- Overcoming the Doubt: Distraction is a natural part of meditation, especially in the beginning. Instead of seeing it as a failure, recognize that noticing distraction is a key part of the practice. Each time you notice your mind wandering and gently bring it back, you're building your mindfulness muscles.

By addressing these doubts and misconceptions with compassion and understanding, you can overcome them and continue to cultivate a meaningful mindfulness practice. Remember, mindfulness is a journey, not a destination, and every step you take is valuable.

6.3 Staying Consistent with Your Practice

Consistency is crucial for reaping the benefits of mindfulness, but maintaining a regular practice can be challenging, especially when life gets busy or distractions arise. Here are some strategies to help you stay consistent with your mindfulness practice:

Strategies for Staying Consistent:

Set Realistic Goals:

- Start with small, achievable goals for your mindfulness practice. For example, commit to practicing for just 5-10 minutes each day, rather than setting an unrealistic goal that might lead to frustration or burnout.
- As you build your practice, gradually increase the duration and variety of mindfulness activities to keep it engaging and fulfilling.

Create a Routine:

- Establish a regular time and place for your mindfulness practice. Whether it's first thing in the morning, during your lunch break, or before bed, having a set routine can help make mindfulness a habit.
- Consider linking your mindfulness practice to an existing habit, such as brushing your teeth or making your morning coffee. This can make it easier to remember and stick to your practice.

Use Reminders and Cues:

- Set reminders on your phone, place sticky notes in visible places, or use a mindfulness app to prompt you to practice mindfulness throughout the day.
- These cues can help you stay on track, especially when you're busy or preoccupied with other tasks.

Find an Accountability Partner:

- Consider practicing mindfulness with a friend or joining a mindfulness group. Having someone to share your experiences with and hold you accountable can provide motivation and support.

- Check in with your accountability partner regularly to discuss your progress, challenges, and any insights you've gained.

Be Flexible and Adaptable:

- Life can be unpredictable, and it's important to be flexible with your mindfulness practice. If you miss a day or need to adjust your routine, don't be too hard on yourself. Simply return to your practice the next day.
- Adapt your practice to fit your current circumstances. If you're traveling, for example, you might practice mindful walking or mindful breathing while on the go.

Reflect on Your Progress:

- Take time to regularly reflect on your mindfulness journey. Consider what's working well and what challenges you've faced. Reflecting on the benefits you've experienced—such as reduced stress, improved focus, or greater emotional balance—can reinforce your commitment to the practice.
- Use your reflections to make adjustments to your routine and set new goals for your mindfulness practice.

Practice Self-Compassion:

- Mindfulness is about being kind and compassionate to yourself, so it's important to extend that kindness to your practice. If you struggle with consistency, remind yourself that it's okay to have ups and downs. What matters is your intention and effort.
- Approach your mindfulness practice with curiosity and a sense

of exploration, rather than rigid expectations. Allow yourself to enjoy the journey, knowing that every moment of mindfulness counts.

By staying consistent with your mindfulness practice, you'll be able to cultivate the full range of benefits that mindfulness offers. Over time, mindfulness will become a natural and integral part of your daily life, supporting your well-being and helping you navigate life's challenges with greater ease.

Chapter 7: Mindfulness and Long-Term Growth

Mindfulness is not just a temporary practice; it's a lifelong journey that can lead to profound personal growth and transformation. In this chapter, we'll explore how mindfulness can help you develop essential qualities like patience and resilience, support your journey toward self-acceptance, and provide tools for continued growth throughout your life. Embracing mindfulness as a long-term practice can bring lasting peace, clarity, and fulfillment.

7.1 Developing Patience and Resilience

Patience and resilience are two qualities that can greatly enhance your ability to navigate life's challenges with grace and strength. Mindfulness plays a crucial role in cultivating these qualities, helping you respond to difficulties with a calm and centered mind.

The Role of Mindfulness in Developing Patience:

Patience is the ability to stay calm and composed, even in the face of delay, difficulty, or frustration. In a world that often demands instant results, cultivating patience can be challenging. However, mindfulness offers a powerful way to develop this important quality.

When you practice mindfulness, you learn to observe your thoughts, emotions, and physical sensations without immediately reacting to them. This creates a space between stimulus and response, allowing you to choose how to respond rather than reacting impulsively. Over time, this practice of pausing and observing can help you develop greater patience.

For example, if you're stuck in traffic or waiting in a long line, mindfulness can help you stay present and avoid becoming frustrated. By focusing on your breath or bringing your attention to the sights and sounds around you, you can shift your perspective and find a sense of calm even in situations that might normally test your patience.

The Role of Mindfulness in Building Resilience:

Resilience is the ability to bounce back from adversity and adapt to change. Life is full of challenges, and resilience is what allows you to face these challenges with strength and perseverance. Mindfulness supports resilience by helping you stay grounded and centered, even when life feels overwhelming.

Mindfulness encourages you to accept your experiences as they are, without resisting or denying them. This acceptance allows you to face difficulties with a clear mind, rather than becoming overwhelmed by negative emotions. By staying present and aware, you can approach challenges with a sense of curiosity and openness, which fosters resilience.

Additionally, mindfulness helps you build resilience by enhancing your emotional regulation. When you're able to manage your emotions effectively, you're better equipped to handle stress, setbacks, and uncertainty. Mindfulness also encourages self-compassion, which is a key component of resilience. By treating yourself with kindness and understanding, you can recover more quickly from setbacks and continue moving forward.

Practices for Cultivating Patience and Resilience:

Mindful Breathing in Difficult Moments:

- When you're feeling impatient or overwhelmed, take a few

moments to focus on your breath. Inhale deeply and exhale slowly, allowing your body and mind to relax.

- As you breathe, remind yourself that it's okay to take things one step at a time. Patience and resilience are built through small, consistent efforts.

Practice Acceptance:

- When faced with a challenge, practice accepting the situation as it is, without trying to change or resist it. Acknowledge your feelings and thoughts, and allow them to be there without judgment.
- Acceptance doesn't mean giving up—it means approaching the situation with a clear mind and an open heart, which can lead to more effective problem-solving and greater resilience.

Reflect on Past Challenges:

- Take time to reflect on past challenges you've faced and how you've overcome them. Recognize the patience and resilience you've already developed, and use these experiences as reminders of your inner strength.
- Consider journaling about your experiences, focusing on what you've learned and how you've grown.

Cultivate Self-Compassion:

- Treat yourself with kindness and understanding, especially during difficult times. Remind yourself that it's okay to struggle and that setbacks are a natural part of life.
- Use loving-kindness meditation to extend compassion to yourself, reinforcing your resilience and patience.

By incorporating mindfulness into your daily life, you can cultivate the patience and resilience needed to navigate life's challenges with greater ease and confidence. These qualities will not only enhance your well-being but also support your long-term growth and success.

7.2 The Journey to Self-Acceptance

Self-acceptance is the foundation of a healthy and fulfilling life. It involves embracing all aspects of yourself—your strengths and weaknesses, your successes and failures—without judgment or self-criticism. Mindfulness is a powerful tool for cultivating self-acceptance, helping you develop a more compassionate and realistic view of yourself.

The Role of Mindfulness in Self-Acceptance:

Mindfulness teaches you to observe your thoughts, emotions, and behaviors without judgment. This non-judgmental awareness is key to self-acceptance, as it allows you to see yourself clearly and honestly, without the distortion of self-criticism or negative beliefs.

Through mindfulness, you learn to recognize and acknowledge your thoughts and feelings without becoming attached to them. This detachment helps you see that your thoughts and emotions are not who you are—they are simply experiences that come and go. By observing these experiences with curiosity and openness, you can develop a more balanced and compassionate view of yourself.

Mindfulness also encourages self-compassion, which is a crucial component of self-acceptance. When you practice self-compassion, you treat yourself with the same kindness and understanding that you would offer to a close friend. This shift in perspective can help you move away from harsh self-criticism and toward a more supportive and nurturing relationship with yourself.

Practices for Cultivating Self-Acceptance:

Mindful Self-Reflection:

- Set aside time each day to reflect on your thoughts, emotions, and behaviors. Observe them without judgment, simply noticing what comes up.
- Ask yourself questions like, "What am I feeling right now?" or "What thoughts are present?" Allow yourself to explore these questions with curiosity and openness.

Practice Self-Compassion:

- When you notice self-critical thoughts, pause and take a deep breath. Gently remind yourself that it's okay to make mistakes and that you're doing the best you can.
- Use loving-kindness meditation to send kind and compassionate thoughts to yourself. Repeat phrases like, "May I be happy," "May I be healthy," and "May I be at peace."

Embrace Imperfections:

- Acknowledge that no one is perfect, and that imperfections are a natural part of being human. Instead of focusing on what you perceive as flaws, try to see them as opportunities for growth and learning.
- Practice accepting your imperfections with kindness and understanding. Remember that self-acceptance doesn't mean complacency—it means recognizing your worth and potential, even as you strive to improve.

Let Go of Comparisons:

- Avoid comparing yourself to others, as this can lead to feelings of inadequacy or self-doubt. Instead, focus on your own unique journey and the progress you've made.
- Use mindfulness to bring your attention back to the present moment, where you can appreciate your own strengths and achievements without the need for comparison.

Celebrate Your Accomplishments:

- Take time to acknowledge and celebrate your accomplishments, no matter how small. Recognize the effort and dedication you've put into your growth and progress.
- Consider keeping a journal of your successes, where you can reflect on your achievements and the steps you've taken toward self-acceptance.

By practicing mindfulness and self-compassion, you can cultivate a deep sense of self-acceptance. This acceptance will empower you to live authentically, embrace your unique qualities, and approach life with greater confidence and peace.

7.3 Continuing Your Mindfulness Journey

Mindfulness is not a destination, but a continuous journey of growth and discovery. As you continue to practice mindfulness, you'll find that it deepens and evolves over time, offering new insights and benefits. Embracing mindfulness as a lifelong practice can lead to lasting transformation and a greater sense of fulfillment.

Tips for Continuing Your Mindfulness Journey:

Stay Open to Growth:

- Approach your mindfulness practice with a sense of curiosity and openness. Recognize that there is always more to learn and explore, and be willing to adapt your practice as you grow.

- Stay open to new experiences, techniques, and perspectives that can enhance your understanding of mindfulness and support your continued growth.

Seek Out Learning Opportunities:

- Consider attending mindfulness workshops, retreats, or courses to deepen your practice and connect with others who share your interest in mindfulness.
- Explore books, podcasts, and online resources that offer new insights and guidance on mindfulness. Continuous learning can keep your practice fresh and engaging.

Reflect on Your Progress:

- Take time regularly to reflect on your mindfulness journey. Consider how your practice has evolved, what challenges you've faced, and what benefits you've experienced.
- Use these reflections to set new goals for your practice and to celebrate the progress you've made.

Integrate Mindfulness into All Areas of Your Life:

- Look for ways to bring mindfulness into all aspects of your life, from your relationships and work to your hobbies and daily routines. The more you integrate mindfulness into your life, the more it becomes a natural and seamless part of who you are.
- Practice mindfulness not only during formal meditation but also in everyday activities, such as eating, walking, and communicating with others.

Connect with a Community:

- Consider joining a mindfulness community or group where you can share your experiences, learn from others, and receive support. Practicing mindfulness with others can provide motivation and encouragement, as well as a sense of belonging.
- If there's no local group available, consider joining an online mindfulness community where you can connect with like-minded individuals.

Embrace Challenges as Opportunities:

- Recognize that challenges are a natural part of the mindfulness journey. When you encounter difficulties, view them as opportunities for growth and learning.
- Use mindfulness to stay present and compassionate with yourself during challenging times, and trust that these experiences will help you deepen your practice.

Cultivate a Lifelong Practice:

- Mindfulness is a practice that can continue to grow and evolve throughout your life. As you move through different stages of life, your practice may take on new forms and meanings.
- Embrace mindfulness as a lifelong journey, and commit to staying present, curious, and open to the unfolding of your practice.

By continuing your mindfulness journey with an open heart and mind, you can experience ongoing growth and transformation. Mindfulness can be a source of strength, peace, and fulfillment throughout your life, supporting you in every step of your journey.

Chapter 8: Embracing a Mindful Life

As we conclude this journey into mindfulness, it's time to reflect on the insights and tools you've gained and consider how you can continue to embrace mindfulness as a way of life. This chapter will recap the key takeaways from the book, offer encouragement for integrating mindfulness into your daily routine, and provide final thoughts on living a mindful life. Mindfulness is not just a practice; it's a path to a more peaceful, fulfilled, and connected existence.

8.1 Reflecting on Your Progress

As you reach the end of this book, it's important to take a moment to reflect on the progress you've made in your mindfulness journey. Whether you've been practicing mindfulness for a while or are just beginning, each step you've taken is valuable and worth acknowledging.

Key Takeaways:

Understanding Mindfulness:

- You've learned that mindfulness is about being fully present in the moment, with an attitude of openness and non-judgment. This simple yet profound practice can help you navigate life's challenges with greater ease and clarity.

Mindfulness Techniques:

- You've explored various mindfulness techniques, such as mindful breathing, body scan meditation, mindful walking, and loving-kindness meditation. These practices offer different ways to cultivate mindfulness and can be integrated into your daily life.

The Benefits of Mindfulness:

- You've discovered the many benefits of mindfulness, including reduced stress and anxiety, enhanced focus and mental clarity, improved emotional regulation, and overall well-being. These benefits highlight the transformative power of mindfulness.

Integrating Mindfulness into Daily Life:

- You've learned how to bring mindfulness into everyday activities, such as eating, working, and interacting with others. By making mindfulness a natural part of your routine, you can experience its benefits throughout the day.

Overcoming Challenges:

- You've addressed common challenges in mindfulness practice, such as restlessness, distraction, doubt, and inconsistency. By applying the strategies provided, you can continue to deepen your practice and overcome obstacles.

Long-Term Growth:

- You've explored how mindfulness supports long-term growth, helping you develop qualities like patience, resilience, and self-acceptance. Embracing mindfulness as a lifelong journey can lead to lasting peace and fulfillment.

Reflecting on Your Journey:

- Take a moment to consider how mindfulness has impacted your life so far. What changes have you noticed in your thoughts, emotions, and behaviors? How has mindfulness helped you navigate challenges or find greater peace and clarity?

- Reflect on the mindfulness practices that resonate most with you. Which techniques have you found most beneficial, and how can you continue to incorporate them into your routine?
- Acknowledge the progress you've made, no matter how small. Every moment of mindfulness is a step forward on your journey.

8.2 Mindfulness as a Lifelong Practice

Mindfulness is not a quick fix or a temporary solution—it's a lifelong practice that evolves and deepens over time. By committing to mindfulness as a way of life, you can continue to grow, learn, and experience its benefits in new and profound ways.

Embracing Mindfulness as a Lifelong Practice:

Cultivate a Daily Routine:

- Continue to make mindfulness a part of your daily routine, whether through formal meditation or mindful activities. Consistency is key to maintaining and deepening your practice.
- Be flexible and adapt your routine as needed. Life is dynamic, and your mindfulness practice can evolve to fit your changing needs and circumstances.

Stay Curious and Open:

- Approach your mindfulness practice with curiosity and an open mind. Allow yourself to explore new techniques, attend workshops or retreats, and learn from others who are also on the mindfulness journey.
- Remember that there is always more to learn and discover. Mindfulness is a rich and diverse practice with endless opportunities for growth.

Integrate Mindfulness into All Areas of Life:

- Look for ways to bring mindfulness into every aspect of your life, from your work and relationships to your hobbies and self-care routines. The more you integrate mindfulness, the more it becomes a natural and effortless part of who you are.
- Use mindfulness to enhance your connections with others, approach challenges with clarity, and find joy in everyday moments.

Practice Self-Compassion:

- Treat yourself with kindness and compassion as you continue your mindfulness journey. It's natural to have ups and downs, and what matters is your commitment to the practice.
- Embrace mindfulness as a way to care for yourself, nurture your well-being, and live with greater peace and fulfillment.

Celebrate Your Progress:

- Take time to celebrate your progress and the positive changes you've experienced through mindfulness. Acknowledge the growth you've achieved and the effort you've put into your practice.
- Share your mindfulness journey with others, whether by teaching, mentoring, or simply sharing your experiences. By doing so, you can inspire others to embrace mindfulness as well.

A Mindful Life:

- As you continue your mindfulness journey, remember that mindfulness is not about reaching a specific destination or achieving a particular goal. It's about being present, moment by moment, and finding peace, clarity, and connection in the here and now.

- Embrace mindfulness as a lifelong companion, one that will support you through life's ups and downs and help you live with greater intention, joy, and fulfillment.

8.3 Final Thoughts and Encouragement

Mindfulness is a journey—one that you've already begun by exploring the practices and insights shared in this book. As you move forward, I encourage you to continue embracing mindfulness with an open heart and mind. The benefits you've experienced so far are just the beginning. With time, patience, and consistent practice, mindfulness can become a transformative force in your life.

Encouragement for Your Journey:

Stay Committed:

- Mindfulness requires ongoing effort, but the rewards are well worth it. Even when life gets busy or challenging, remember to return to your practice. Every moment of mindfulness brings you closer to a more peaceful and fulfilled life.

Be Gentle with Yourself:

- Mindfulness is about self-compassion and non-judgment. If you encounter setbacks or find it difficult to stay consistent, be kind to yourself. Recognize that growth takes time, and every effort you make is valuable.

Keep Learning:

- Mindfulness is a vast and rich field with endless opportunities for exploration. Stay curious and open to new experiences, and continue learning from teachers, books, and your own practice.

Share Your Practice:

- Consider sharing your mindfulness journey with others. Whether through conversation, teaching, or simply leading by example, you can inspire others to embrace mindfulness and experience its benefits.

A Final Word:

As you continue your mindfulness journey, may you find peace, clarity, and fulfillment in every moment. Mindfulness is a gift you give to yourself—a way to live more fully, connect more deeply, and navigate life's challenges with grace and resilience. Thank you for taking this journey with me, and I wish you all the best as you continue to explore the transformative power of mindfulness.

Chapter 9: Further Resources on Mindfulness

Mindfulness is a vast and evolving field with endless opportunities for learning and growth. Whether you're looking to deepen your practice, explore new techniques, or connect with a community, there are many resources available to support your journey. In this chapter, you'll find a curated list of recommended books, articles, online courses, apps, and communities that can help you continue your mindfulness journey.

9.1 Recommended Books and Articles

Reading can be a powerful way to deepen your understanding of mindfulness and explore different perspectives on the practice. Here are some highly recommended books and articles:

Books:

"Wherever You Go, There You Are" by Jon Kabat-Zinn

This classic book by one of the pioneers of mindfulness in the West offers a practical and accessible introduction to mindfulness. It's filled with insights and exercises to help you bring mindfulness into your daily life.

"The Miracle of Mindfulness" by Thich Nhat Hanh

Written by the renowned Vietnamese Buddhist monk Thich Nhat Hanh, this book offers a gentle and profound guide to mindfulness. It's a great resource for those seeking to integrate mindfulness into every aspect of their lives.

"Radical Acceptance" by Tara Brach

Tara Brach's book combines mindfulness with self-compassion, offering a powerful approach to healing and self-acceptance. It's particularly helpful for those who struggle with self-criticism or feelings of inadequacy.

"The Power of Now" by Eckhart Tolle

Although not strictly about mindfulness, Eckhart Tolle's book emphasizes the importance of living in the present moment, a key aspect of mindfulness. It's a transformative read for those seeking to cultivate deeper presence and awareness.

"Mindfulness in Plain English" by Bhante Henepola Gunaratana

This straightforward and practical guide to mindfulness meditation offers clear instructions and insights for both beginners and experienced practitioners. It's a valuable resource for anyone looking to deepen their meditation practice.

Articles:

"What Is Mindfulness?" by Mindful.org

This article provides a clear and concise overview of mindfulness, its benefits, and how to practice it. It's a great starting point for those new to mindfulness.

"The Science of Mindfulness" by the Greater Good Science Center

This article explores the scientific research behind mindfulness and its impact on mental health, well-being, and overall quality of life.

"How to Practice Mindfulness" by The New York Times

A practical guide to getting started with mindfulness, this article offers tips and techniques for incorporating mindfulness into your daily routine.

"The Benefits of Mindfulness" by the American Psychological Association

This article summarizes the psychological benefits of mindfulness, including its effects on stress reduction, emotional regulation, and cognitive function.

9.2 Online Courses and Apps for Mindfulness

If you're interested in structured learning or guided practice, online courses and mindfulness apps can be excellent resources. Here are some options:

Online Courses:

"Mindfulness-Based Stress Reduction (MBSR)" by Jon Kabat-Zinn (Available on various platforms)

This 8-week online course is based on the MBSR program developed by Jon Kabat-Zinn. It's one of the most well-known and respected mindfulness programs, designed to help you reduce stress and cultivate greater awareness.

"The Science of Well-Being" by Yale University (Available on Coursera)

While not solely focused on mindfulness, this popular course covers various aspects of well-being, including mindfulness practices. It's a great resource for those looking to enhance their overall happiness and mental health.

"Mindful Meditation" by Tara Brach (Available on TaraBrach.com and various platforms)

Tara Brach offers a variety of online courses and guided meditations focused on mindfulness, self-compassion, and emotional healing. Her teachings are accessible and deeply transformative.

"Introduction to Mindfulness" by The School of Life (Available on TheSchoolofLife.com)

This course offers a practical introduction to mindfulness, exploring its benefits and how to incorporate it into your daily life. It's a great option for beginners.

Mindfulness Apps:

Headspace:

Headspace offers guided meditations, mindfulness exercises, and courses tailored to different needs, such as stress reduction, sleep improvement, and focus enhancement. The app is user-friendly and great for beginners.

Calm:

Calm provides a wide range of guided meditations, sleep stories, and mindfulness programs. It's known for its soothing interface and diverse content, making it suitable for all levels of practice.

Insight Timer:

Insight Timer is a free app with a large library of guided meditations from teachers around the world. It also includes a customizable meditation timer and features for tracking your practice.

10% Happier:

Based on the book by Dan Harris, this app offers practical mindfulness and meditation techniques, with a focus on making mindfulness accessible and relatable. It's a great choice for those who prefer a down-to-earth approach.

9.3 Mindfulness Retreats and Workshops

Attending a mindfulness retreat or workshop can be a powerful way to deepen your practice and connect with others who share your interest in mindfulness. Here are some options:

Mindfulness Retreats:

Spirit Rock Meditation Center (California, USA):

Spirit Rock offers a variety of mindfulness and meditation retreats, ranging from weekend programs to extended silent retreats. It's a beautiful and serene environment ideal for deepening your practice.

Plum Village (France):

Founded by Thich Nhat Hanh, Plum Village offers retreats focused on mindfulness, peace, and community living. It's a unique opportunity to immerse yourself in mindful living in a supportive environment.

The Omega Institute (New York, USA):

The Omega Institute offers a range of mindfulness workshops and retreats, led by experienced teachers. The center is known for its peaceful setting and diverse programming.

Insight Meditation Society (Massachusetts, USA):

The Insight Meditation Society offers silent retreats that emphasize Vipassana (insight) meditation. It's a wonderful place to deepen your mindfulness practice and experience the benefits of sustained meditation.

Workshops:

Mindfulness Workshops by Mindful.org:

Mindful.org offers various online and in-person workshops on mindfulness, covering topics like stress reduction, mindful parenting, and workplace mindfulness. These workshops are led by experienced instructors and are accessible to all levels.

Google's "Search Inside Yourself" Program:

Originally developed at Google, this program combines mindfulness with emotional intelligence training. It's offered in various locations and online, making it accessible to a wide audience.

Kripalu Center for Yoga & Health (Massachusetts, USA):

Kripalu offers workshops on mindfulness, meditation, and holistic health. The center's peaceful environment and experienced teachers make it an ideal setting for deepening your practice.

9.4 Communities and Support Groups

Connecting with others who share your interest in mindfulness can provide valuable support, motivation, and inspiration. Here are some ways to find mindfulness communities and support groups:

Online Communities:

The Mindfulness Community on Reddit (r/Mindfulness):

This active subreddit is a place where people from around the world share their experiences, ask questions, and offer support related to mindfulness practice.

Insight Timer Community:

The Insight Timer app includes a community feature where users can join groups, participate in discussions, and connect with others who are practicing mindfulness.

Mindful.org Community:

Mindful.org offers an online community where members can connect, share resources, and participate in discussions about mindfulness. It's a supportive space for those looking to deepen their practice.

Facebook Groups:

There are many Facebook groups dedicated to mindfulness and meditation, where members share resources, experiences, and encouragement. Simply search for "mindfulness" or "meditation" groups on Facebook to find a community that resonates with you.

In-Person Groups:

Local Meditation Centers:

Many cities have meditation centers that offer group meditation sessions, mindfulness classes, and community events. These centers often provide a welcoming environment for both beginners and experienced practitioners.

Mindfulness-Based Stress Reduction (MBSR) Groups:

MBSR programs are offered in various locations worldwide, often through hospitals, wellness centers, and universities. These groups provide structured mindfulness training and the opportunity to connect with others.

Yoga Studios:

Many yoga studios offer mindfulness and meditation classes in addition to yoga. These classes can be a great way to meet like-minded individuals and deepen your mindfulness practice.

Mindfulness Meetups:

Meetup.com is a platform where people can create and join groups based on shared interests. Search for mindfulness or meditation meetups in your area to find local groups that meet regularly for practice and discussion.

Don't miss out!

Visit the website below and you can sign up to receive emails whenever Shalna Omaye publishes a new book. There's no charge and no obligation.

https://books2read.com/r/B-A-ZAIW-BRJYE

BOOKS 2 READ

Connecting independent readers to independent writers.

Did you love *Mindfulness Made Simple: A Beginner's Guide to Mental Clarity and Peace*? Then you should read *The Art of Emotional Intelligence: Master Your Emotions for Success*[1] by Shalna Omaye!

Unlock the power of emotional intelligence and transform your life with "The Art of Emotional Intelligence: Mastering Your Emotions for Success." This comprehensive guide takes you on a journey to understand and enhance your emotional intelligence, leading to better decision-making, stronger relationships, and greater success in both personal and professional settings.

What You'll Discover:

Introduction to Emotional Intelligence: Learn what emotional intelligence is, why it matters, and how it differs from traditional IQ. **The Core Components of Emotional Intelligence**: Explore the

---

1. https://books2read.com/u/4j7ro2

2. https://books2read.com/u/4j7ro2

essential elements of emotional intelligence, including self-awareness, self-regulation, motivation, empathy, and social skills.**The Science Behind Emotional Intelligence**: Delve into the neurological and psychological mechanisms that drive emotional intelligence, and understand its impact on decision-making and mental health.**Developing Emotional Intelligence:** Gain practical strategies for enhancing your emotional intelligence, from increasing self-awareness to improving social skills.**Emotional Intelligence in the Workplace:** Discover how emotional intelligence can boost your career, improve leadership, and create a more harmonious work environment.**Emotional Intelligence in Personal Relationships**: Learn how to apply emotional intelligence to strengthen your romantic relationships, parenting, friendships, and social interactions.**Challenges and Misconceptions About Emotional Intelligence**: Address common myths and barriers to developing emotional intelligence, and learn how to avoid potential pitfalls.**Embracing a Life of Emotional Intelligence:** Reflect on the long-term benefits of emotional intelligence and get inspired to continue your journey toward a more balanced, fulfilling life.

Whether you're looking to improve your communication skills, enhance your leadership abilities, or simply lead a more emotionally balanced life, this book provides you with the tools and insights needed to master your emotions and achieve your goals.

Also by Shalna Omaye

AI Insights
Mastering Conversation with ChatGPT: A Comprehensive Guide

Financial Advice Detective
A Beginner's Guide to Exchange-Traded Funds (ETFs)

In the Realm of Dreams: Sleep and its Secrets
Whispers of the Night: Illuminating the Enigmatic World of Dreams
The Dream Realm: Exploring the Depths and Dimensions of the
Sleeping Mind

Mindscapes: Navigating the Psyche
Procrastination: Breaking the Habit
The Art of Emotional Intelligence: Master Your Emotions for Success
Mindfulness Made Simple: A Beginner's Guide to Mental Clarity and
Peace

Questing4Answers
Cosmic Chronicles: Unveiling the Wonders of Space
Fueling the Future: Pathway to Sustainability

World Habits, Customs & Traditions
St. Patrick's Day: A Look into the Origins of Ireland's Celebrated
Holiday
Celebrating New Beginnings: Global Traditions of the New Year

Standalone
Valentine's Day: The Strange but True Story